THE
NEW YORKER
BOOK OF ART CARTOONS

THE
NEW YORKER
BOOK OF ART CARTOONS

EDITED BY ROBERT MANKOFF

BLOOMBERG PRESS

NEW YORK

PUBLISHED BY BLOOMBERG PRESS

First edition published 2005
1 3 5 7 9 10 8 6 4 2

Library of Congress Cataloging-in-Publication Data

The New Yorker book of art cartoons / edited by Robert Mankoff.
    p. cm.
   Includes index.
   Summary: "A collection of 117 cartoons on art from The New Yorker magazine in a period ranging from the 1930s to the current decade"--Provided by publisher.
    ISBN 1-57660-129-3 (alk. paper)
   1. Art--Caricatures and cartoons. 2. Artists--Caricatures and cartoons. 3. American wit and humor, Pictorial. 4. New Yorker (New York, N.Y. : 1925) I. Mankoff, Robert. II. New Yorker (New York, N.Y. : 1925)

NC1428 .N47 2005
741.5'973--dc22   2005048156

THE
NEW YORKER
BOOK OF ART CARTOONS

"*I think you know everybody.*"

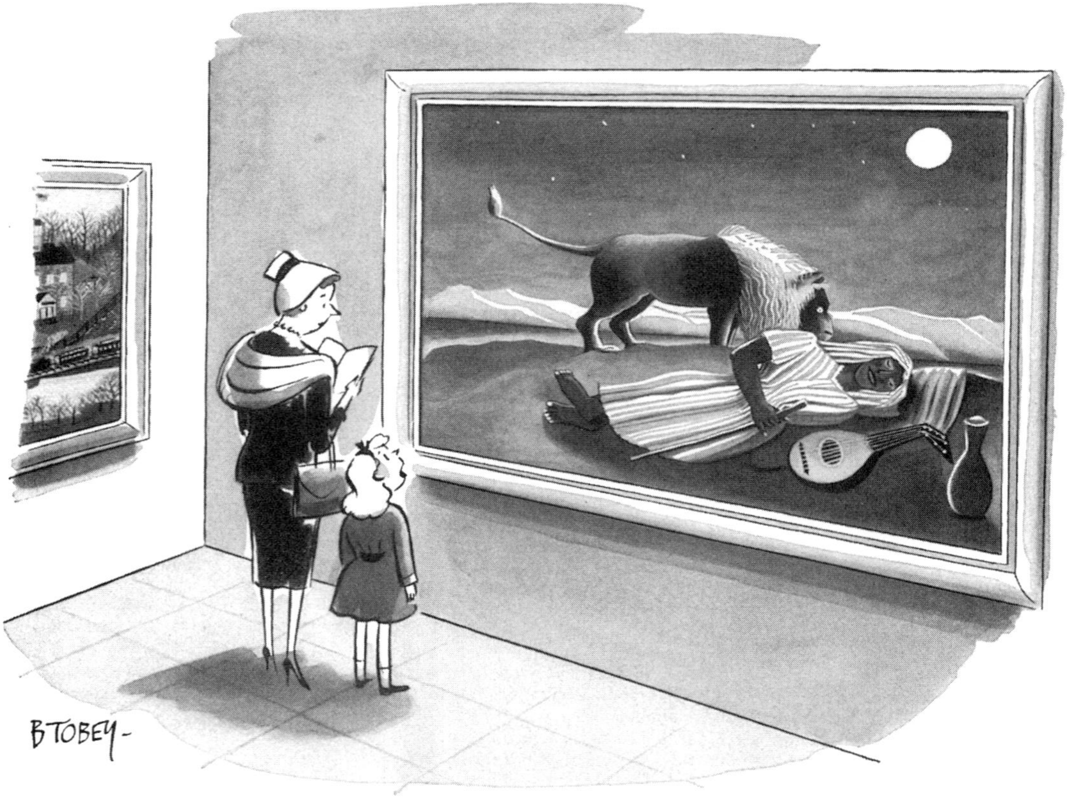
B TOBEY-

"Then what happened?"

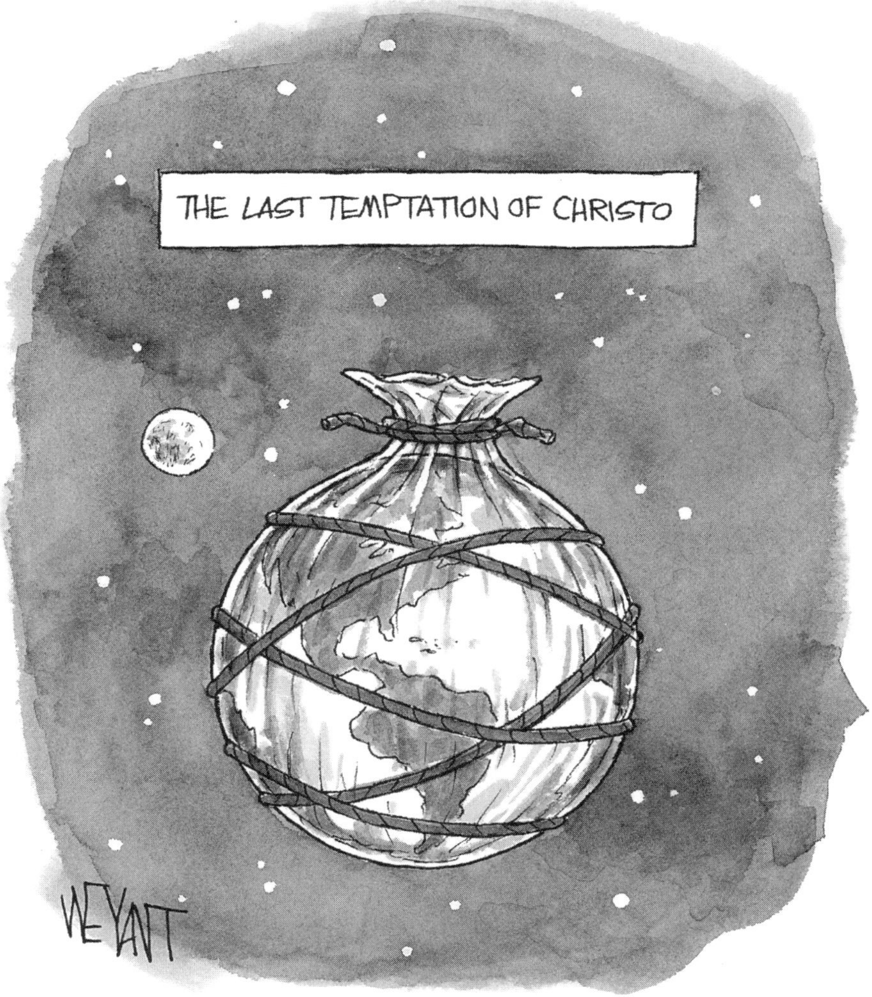
THE LAST TEMPTATION OF CHRISTO
WEYANT

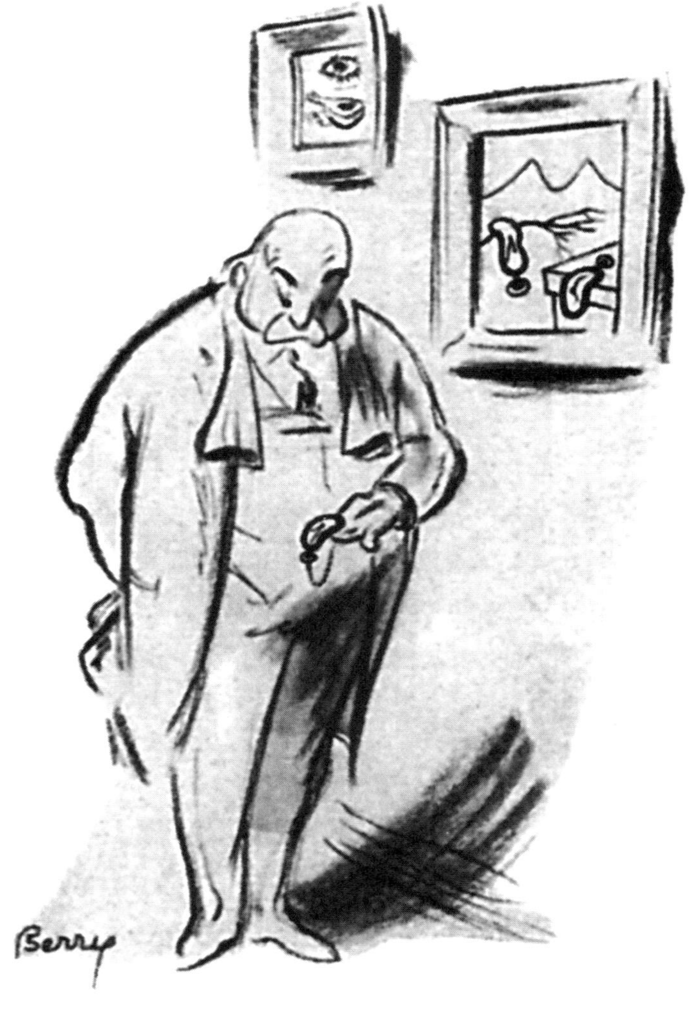
Berry

"Gauguin started at forty!"

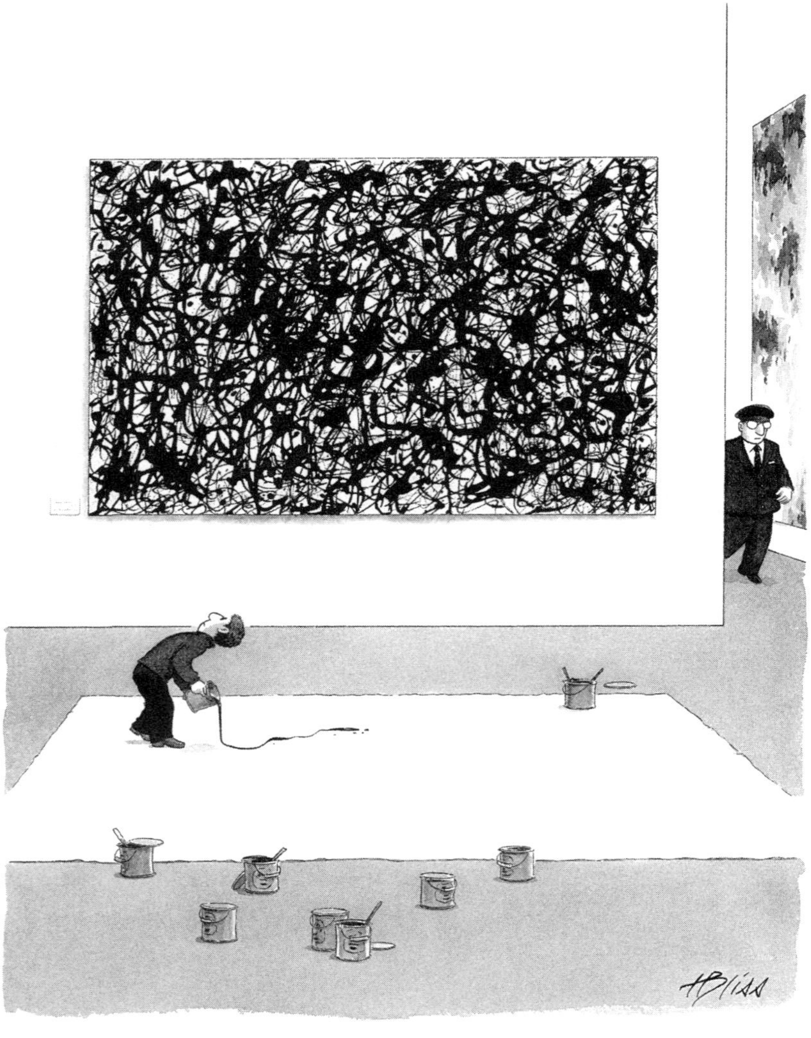
HBliss

"Say, why don't we go see the Hopper show at the Whitney?"

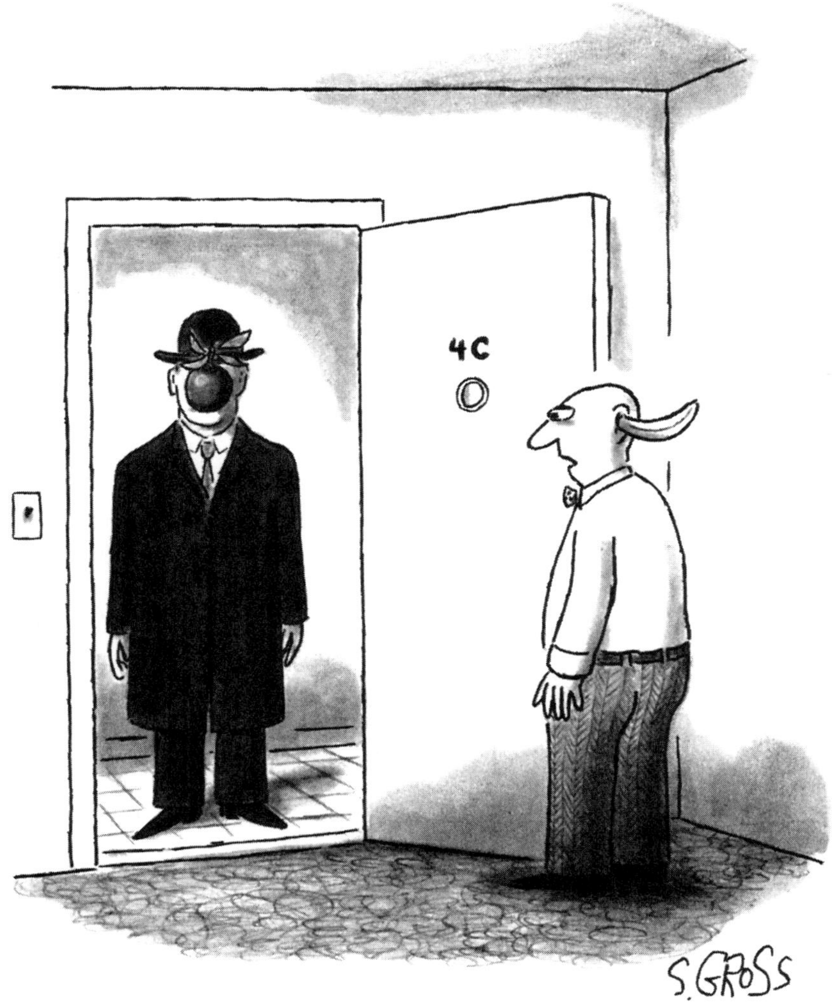
4C
S.GROSS

"Oh, it's you."

"We haven't, of course, but I have the strangest feeling that we've been here before."

"*Fortunately, I think we have an extremely accurate copy of it in the museum's gift shop.*"

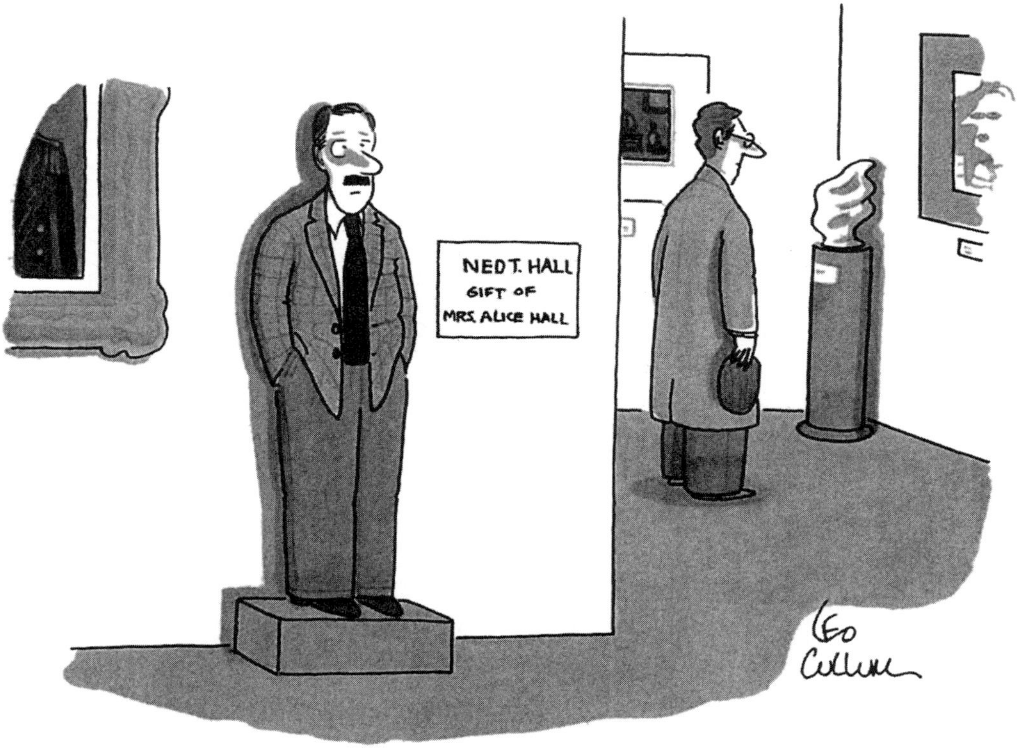
NED T. HALL
GIFT OF
MRS. ALICE HALL

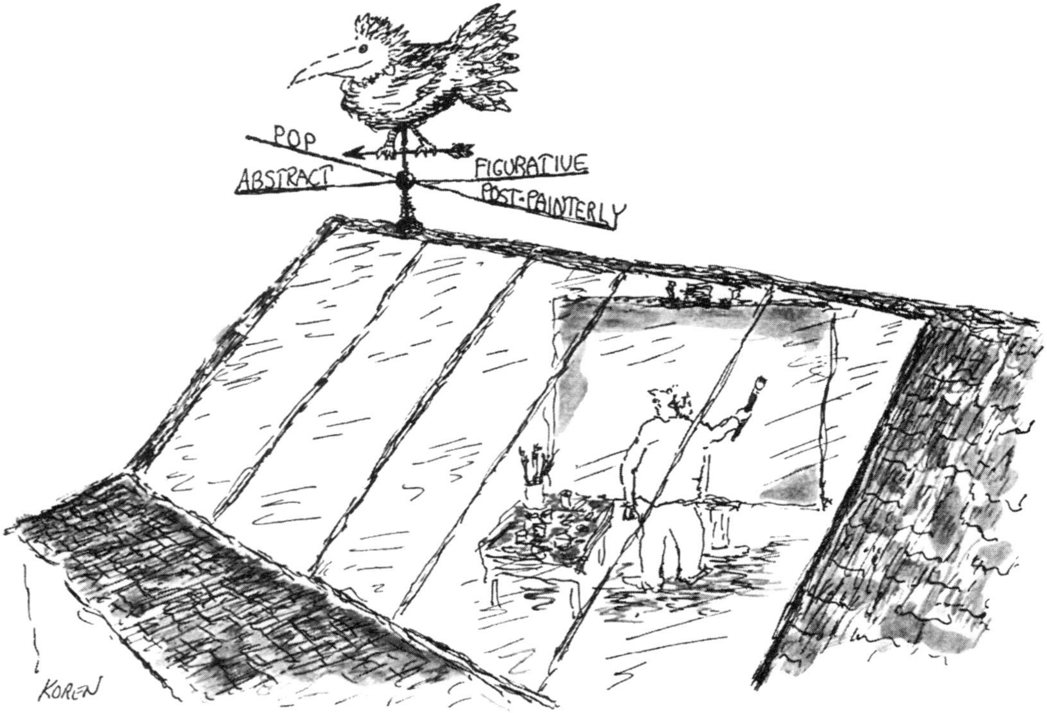
POP
ABSTRACT
FIGURATIVE
POST-PAINTERLY
KOREN

"Tell us again about Monet, Grandpa."

"I'll grant you his work has a certain naïve immediacy."

"We're in Japanese waters, that's for sure."

"The original hangs on the New York State Thruway."

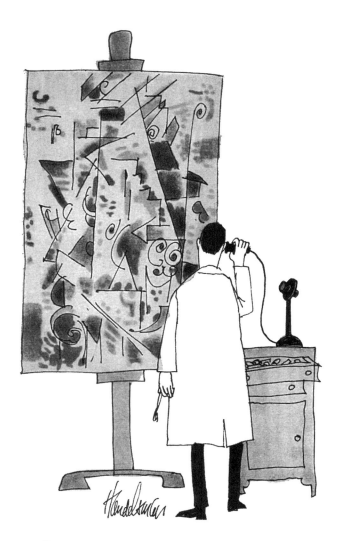

"Hello, Braque? Picasso here. Cubism is out."

"This will give you a rough idea of how it will look."

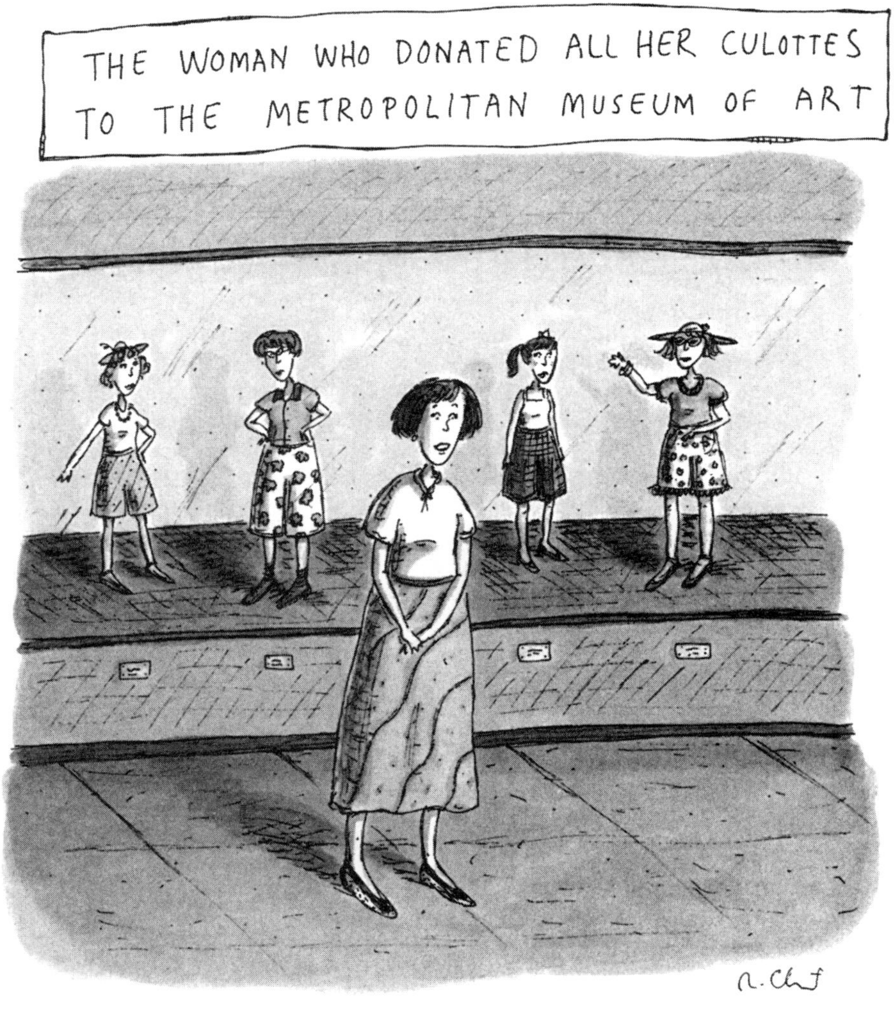
THE WOMAN WHO DONATED ALL HER CULOTTES
TO THE METROPOLITAN MUSEUM OF ART
R. Chast

"*Oh, John, if only we could be sure it's love and not just the spell of this place!*"

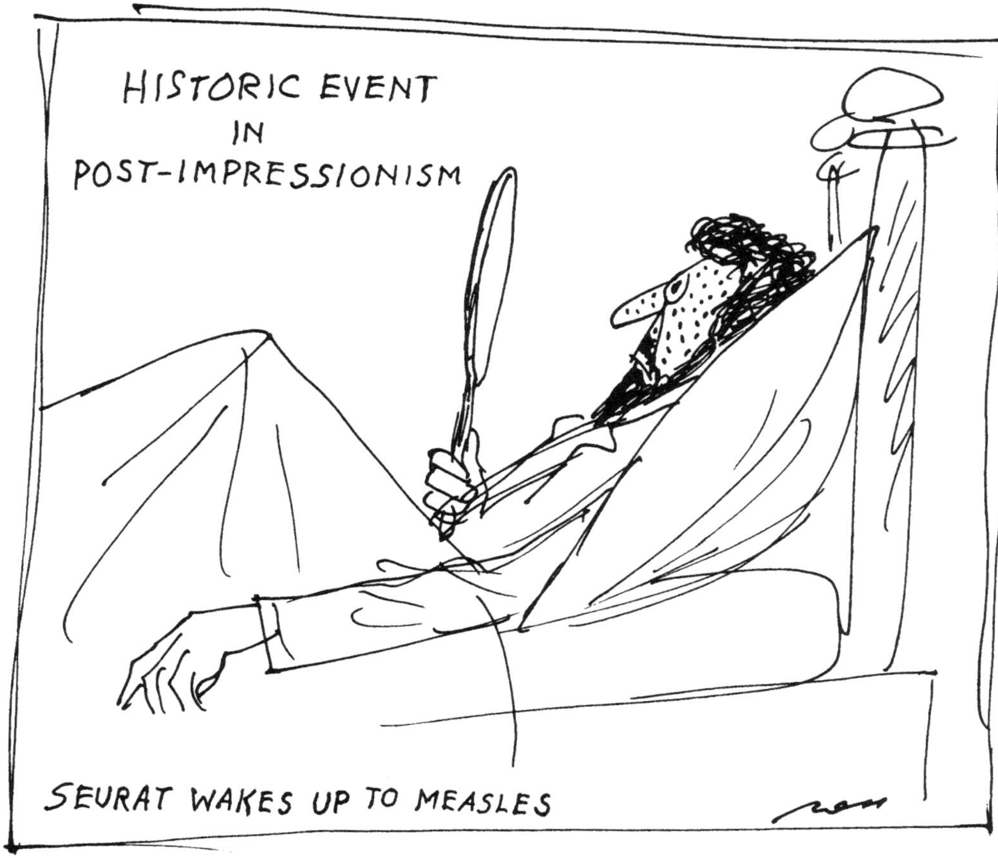
HISTORIC EVENT
IN
POST-IMPRESSIONISM
SEURAT WAKES UP TO MEASLES

GREGORY

"What I do as an artist is to take an ordinary object—say, a lamppost—and, by urinating on it, transform it into something that is uniquely my own."

"*Those old guys really had it!*"

"Frieze!"

NOBODY COMES BETWEEN NANCY & HER MONDRIAN

"This *is* a complete retrospective."

"Careful now. It's fragile."

"And then, in yet another stunning volte-face, the artist rediscovered the human figure."

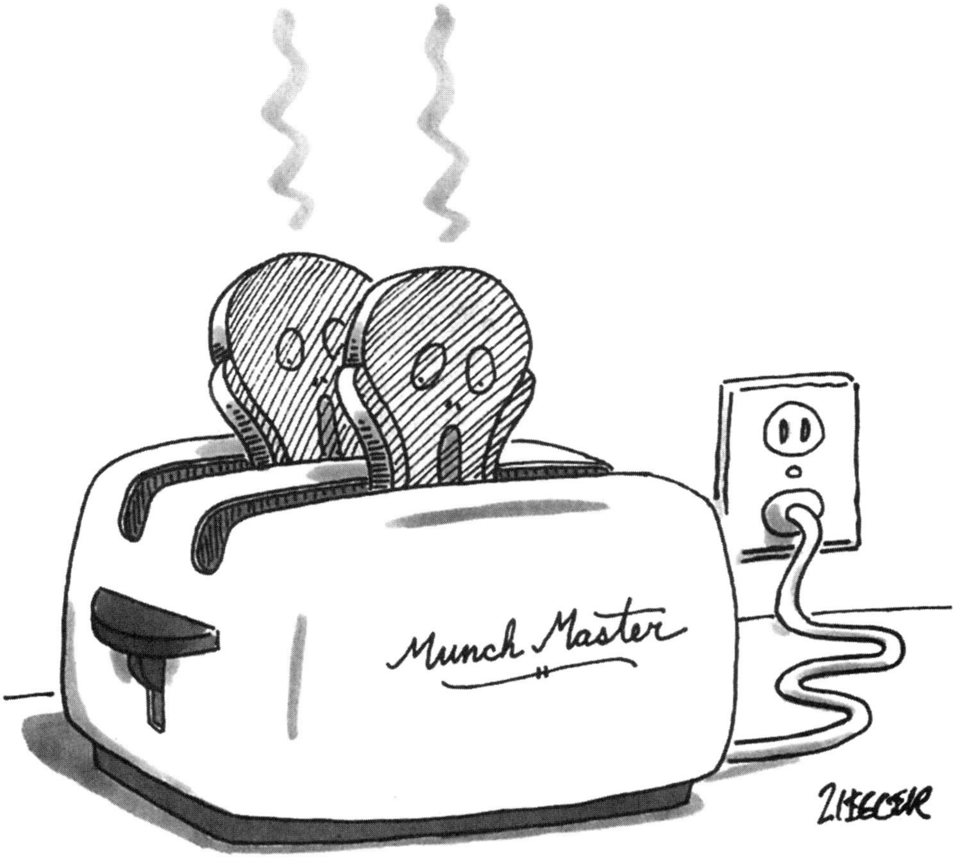
Munch Master
ZIEGLER

"Just because the painting doesn't happen to appeal to Marvin doesn't necessarily mean it stinks."

"That's the Hudson River School, son."

"Well, for that matter, what is the meaning of you?"

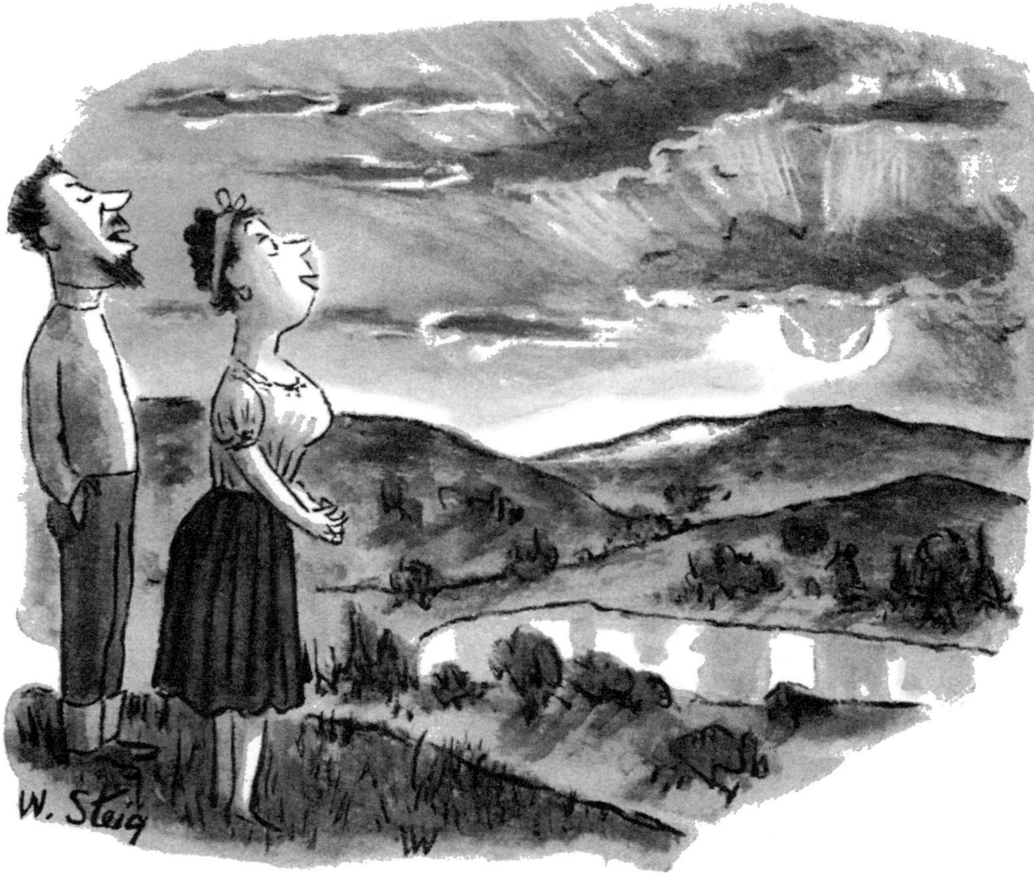
W. Steig

"Too much purple."

"People read too much into everything."

"Well, it was sort of like a cook-out."

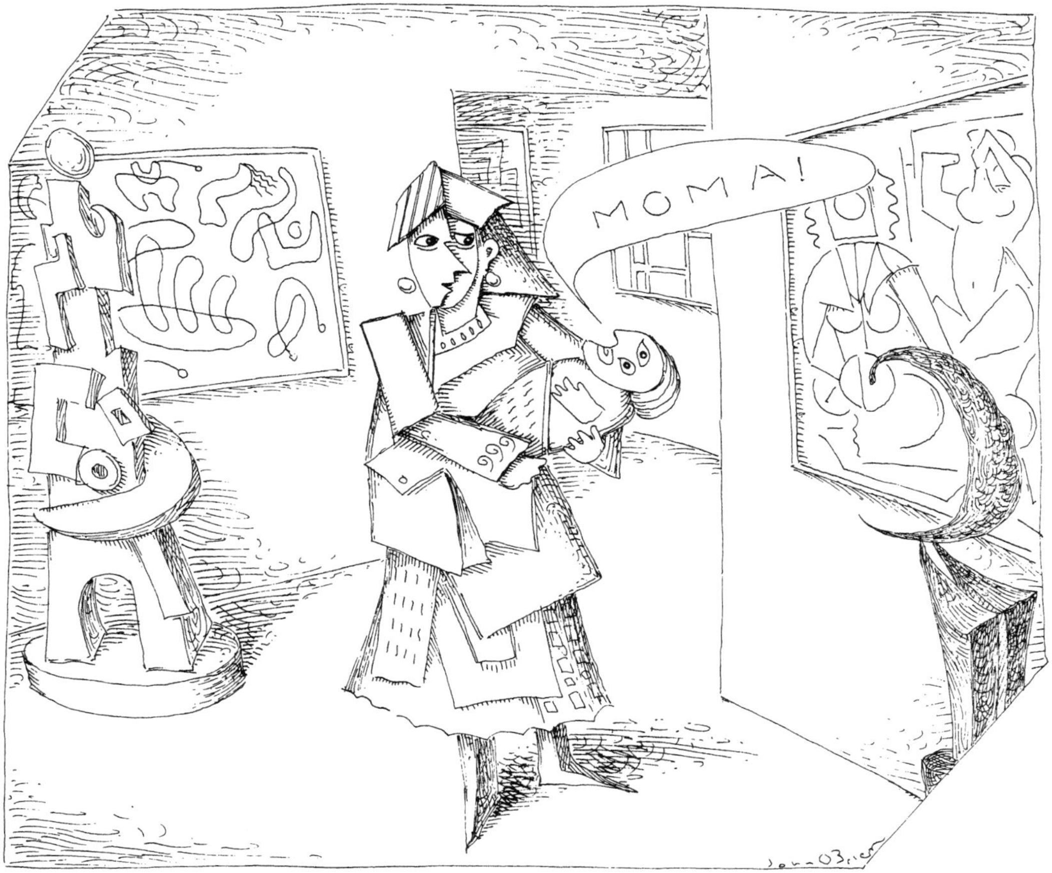
MOMA!

"*I'm not going to be the one to tell 'em it's a ventilator.*"

CAFÉ NOTRE DAME

"I don't think you even __want__ to see the Louvre."

"I guess cats just can't appreciate Frank Gehry."

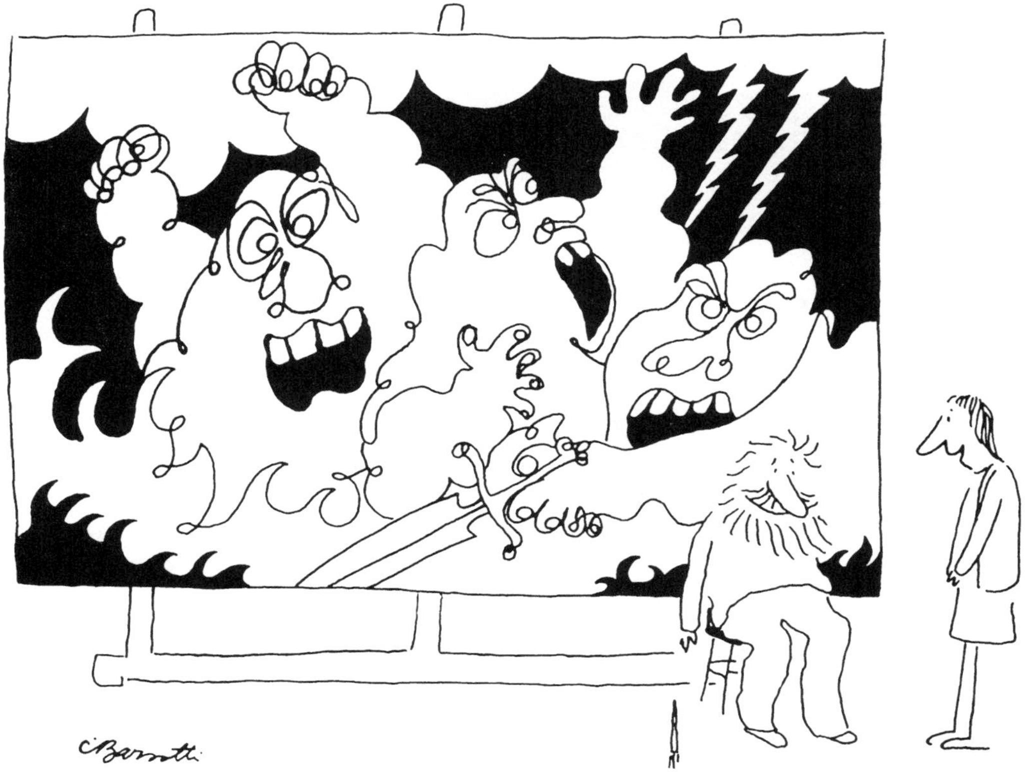
cBarsotti

"Feel better, dear?"

"Time for bed, Anton. You've suffered enough for one day."

"Surely, Son, you can find something to paint indoors."

"Well, it's no wonder those Borgias and Medicis were always poisoning each other."

"I think it was along about here that he slipped a disc."

"Know what I think? I think you're onto something really big."

"George, I don't know how you're going to take this,
but I've grown tired of modern."

"We've already done this room. I remember that fire extinguisher."

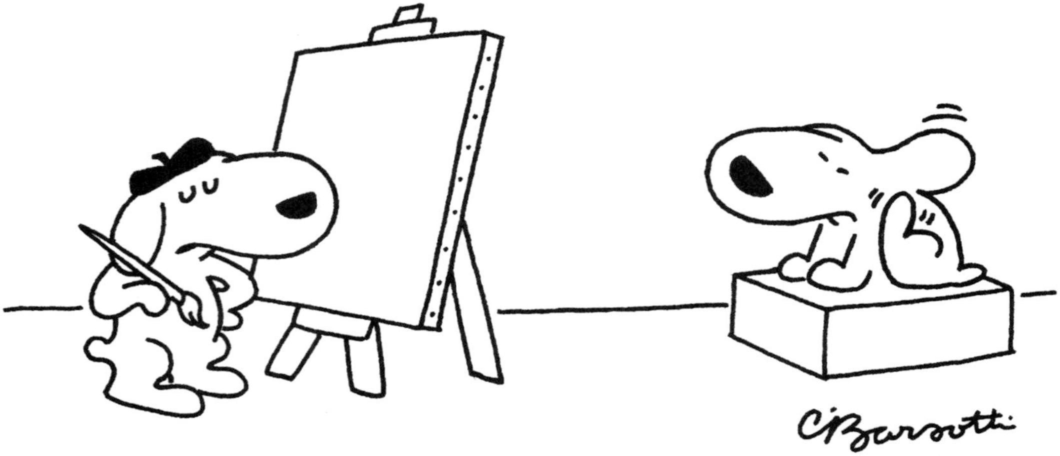

CBarsotti

"Whenver you're ready."

"Are they allowed to do that on Fifth Avenue?"

"The price of one million five is the highest price ever paid for a Blanchard, and represents a three-hundred-per-cent increase in value from its 1970 price of three hundred seventy-five thousand dollars. Prior to 1970, it was owned by the Countess Barasev, who paid one hundred twenty thousand dollars for it in 1952, purchasing it from De Witt Orstlund, who paid sixty-five thousand dollars for it in 1940."

"Here! Let me get you all in!"

"Why, thank you for the compliment, Donald, but I think that will be enough of that."

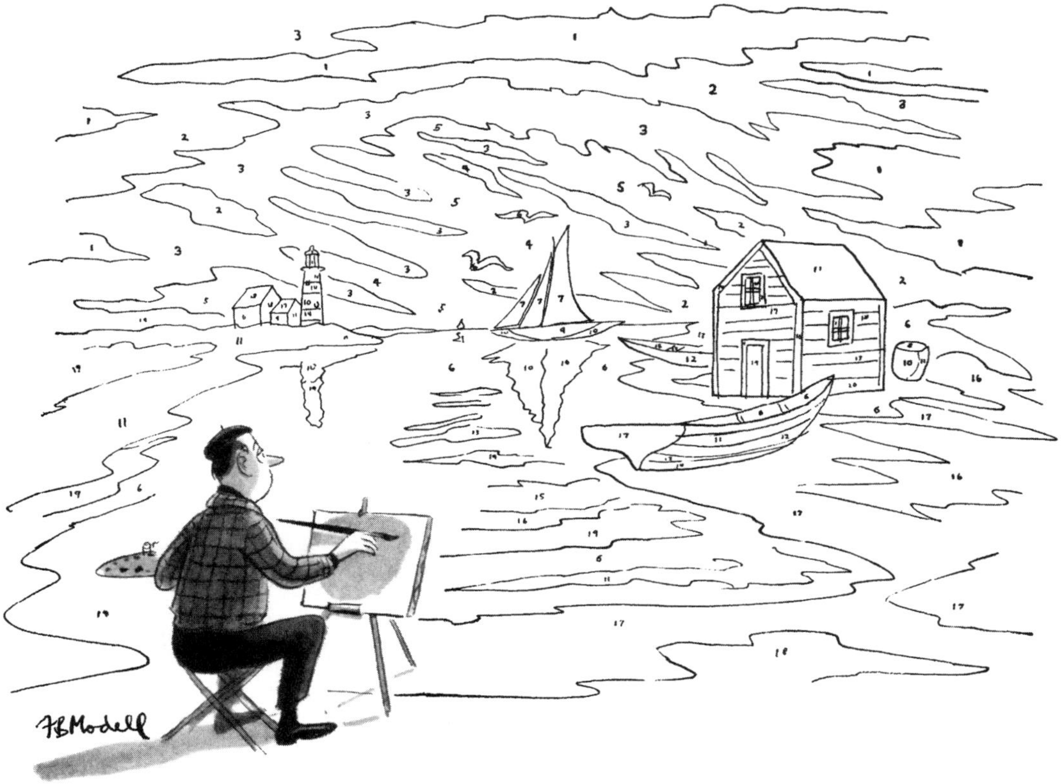
FBModell

"For big, important things, it's the Met and the Modern, of course—
but the Whitney is great for stocking-stuffers."

"*I used to like everything before I took my art-appreciation course.*"

"See? While your unsurpassed collection of gum wrappers sits idle!"

"He begged his wife and kids to join him in Tahiti,
but he didn't mean a word of it, the bastard."

"You rarely see this kind of joy for under ten thousand."

"I see your Granny Smith, and I raise you a Golden Delicious."

"*Roger has always been text-driven.*"

"I know more about art than you do, so I'll tell you what to like."

"Sotheby's extends its deepest sympathies and wonders whether the deceased might have owned any early German Expressionist pieces."

"This painting, we're sorry to say, is pure trash."

"Not bad, for art."

"I feel just like that sometimes."

"Well, this initial test suggests that the authenticity of your Rembrandt may be questionable."

STEINBERG

"Here's one you'll understand."

"Wow! You mean they got all this in exchange for just one van Gogh?"

"I was rather hoping a Passaic River School
might form, but so far it's just me."

"Now, this one is probably way over your head."

"I never can remember. Is it Manet or Monet who
isn't as good as the other?"

"*Someday this cave could be worth plenty.*"

"*This artist is a deeply religious feminist and anti-smoking advocate,
who made a lot of money in the computer industry before going off to paint
in Paris, where she now lives with her husband and two little girls.*"

"Their little minds are busy every minute."

"A million five is the sticker price, so to speak."

"I'm leaving you, Howard. I've followed you from the West Village to the East Village to SoHo to NoHo to BeloHo—but Hoboken is too much."

"I can't imagine bringing a child into the current art world."

"*You're putting in too many people!*"

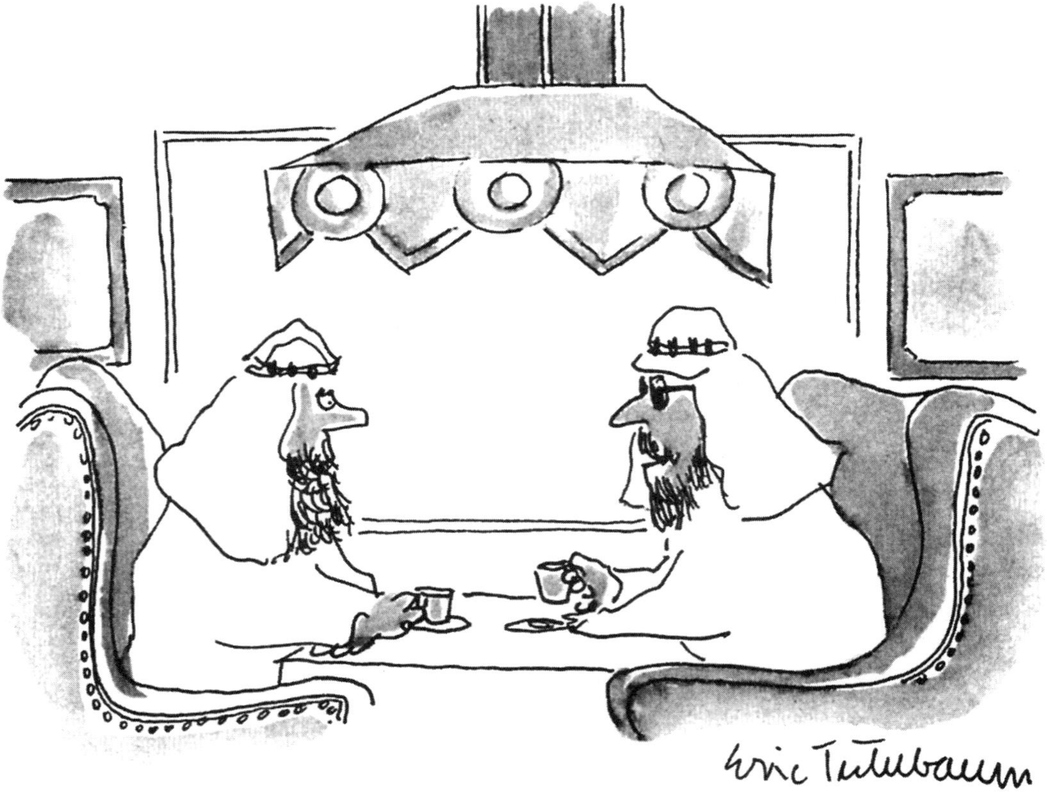
Eric Teitelbaum

"Through it all we're still heavily invested in oil—primarily Picasso and Rembrandt."

"*Is it all right to sneer at these now?*"

"*The edges are nice and hard, but your colors aren't icky enough.*"

"Is that all you can say—'It's not messy'?"

"It must be _pouring_ outside."

"Instead of 'It sucks' you could say, 'It doesn't speak to me.'"

"The moment I saw this, my soul cried out that it could triple in value."

"I hate these one-man shows."

"'Perceptual and kinetic art have an intertwined development that cannot be totally disentangled; nevertheless perceptual, optical, or "virtual" movement—which always exists in tension with factual immobility—is an experience of a different order.'"

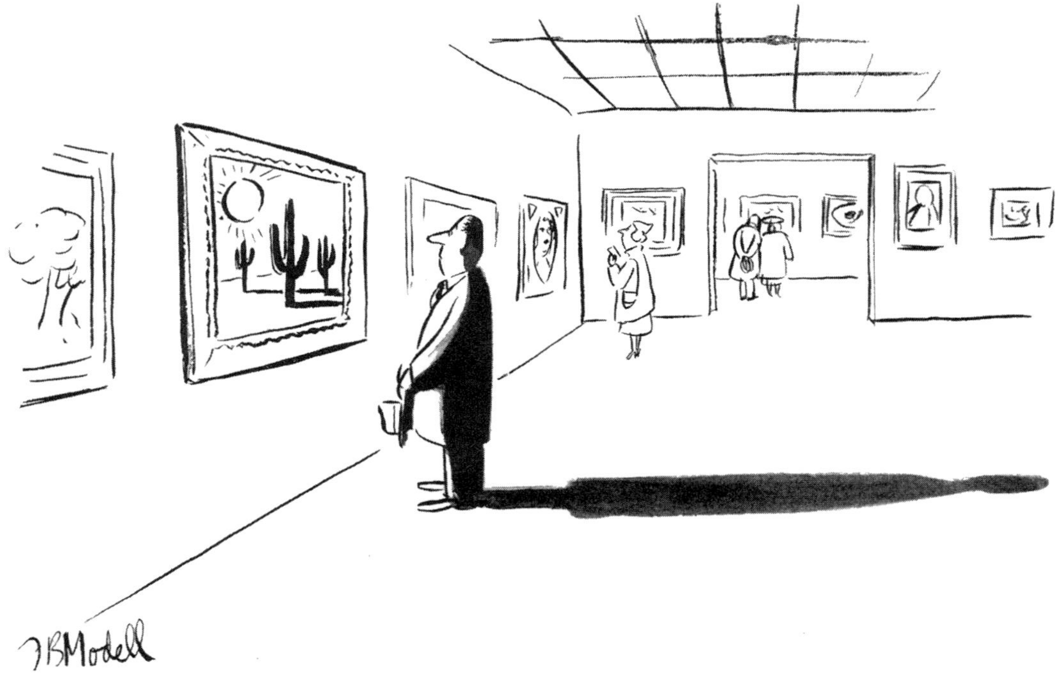
FBModell

"Now tell me about Pop and Op!"

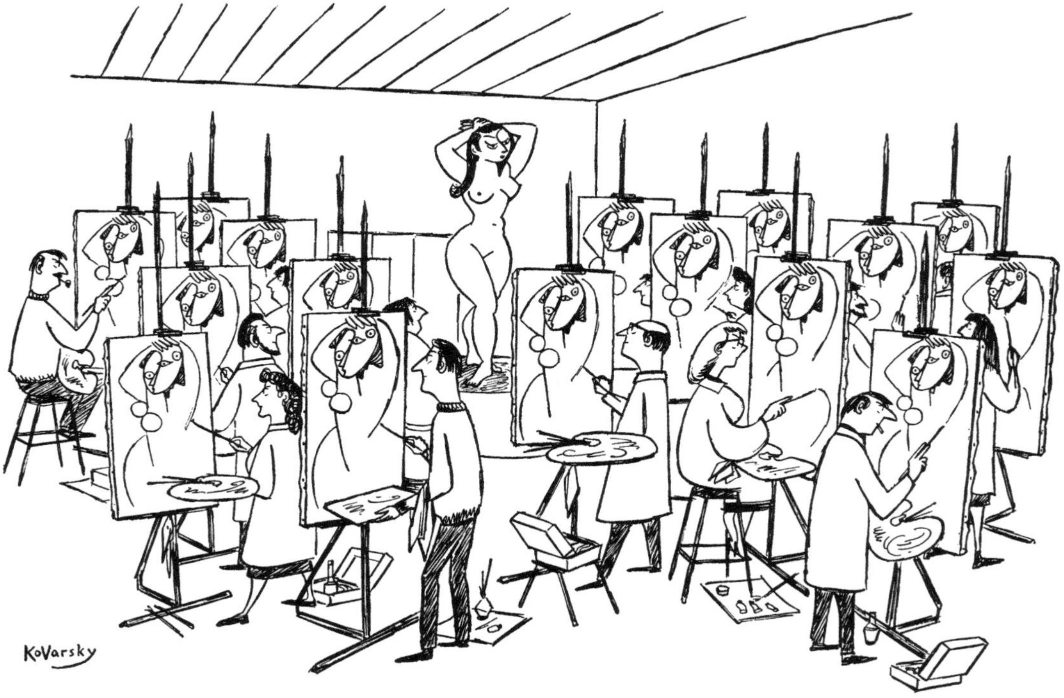
KoVarsky

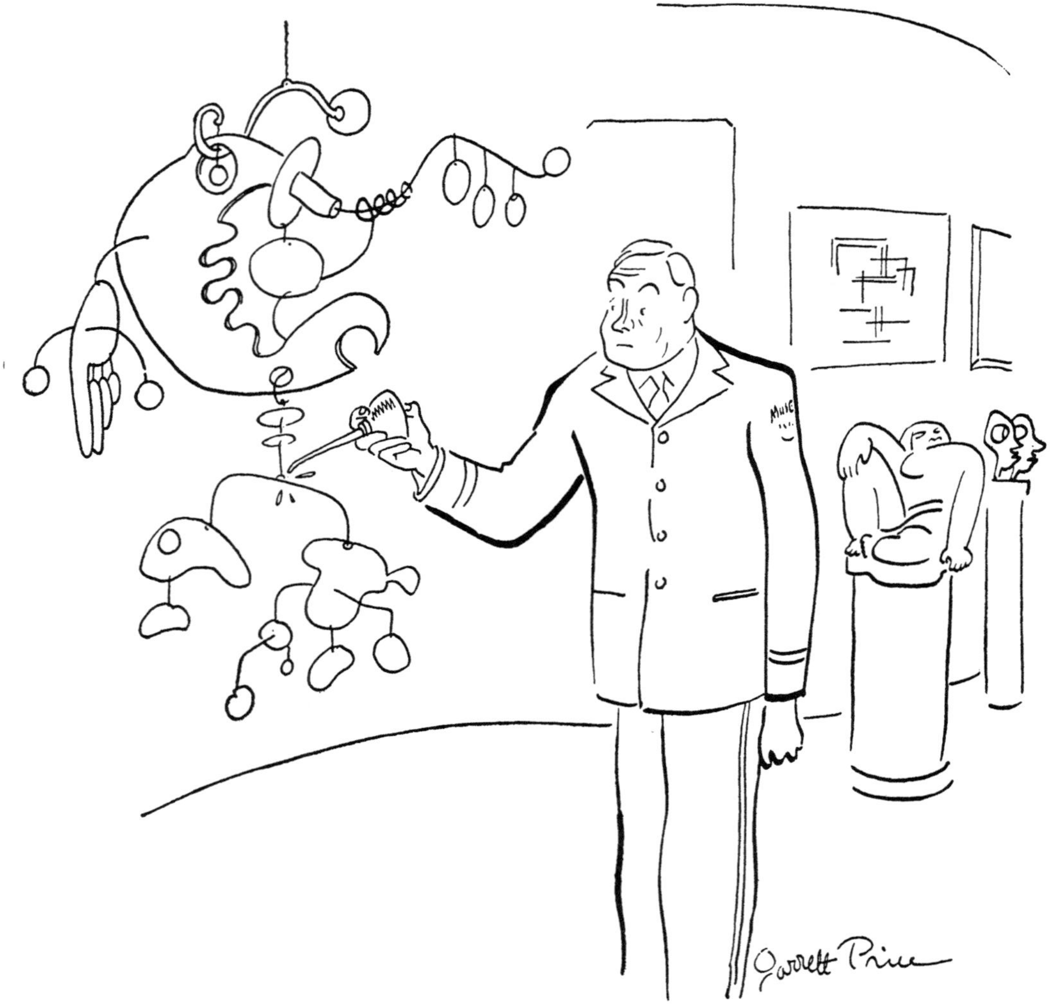
Garrett Price

"I never know how far away to stand to make them look good."

"Which way to the Mona Lisa? We're double-parked."

"The artist lives in Port Jervis, New York, if that helps any."

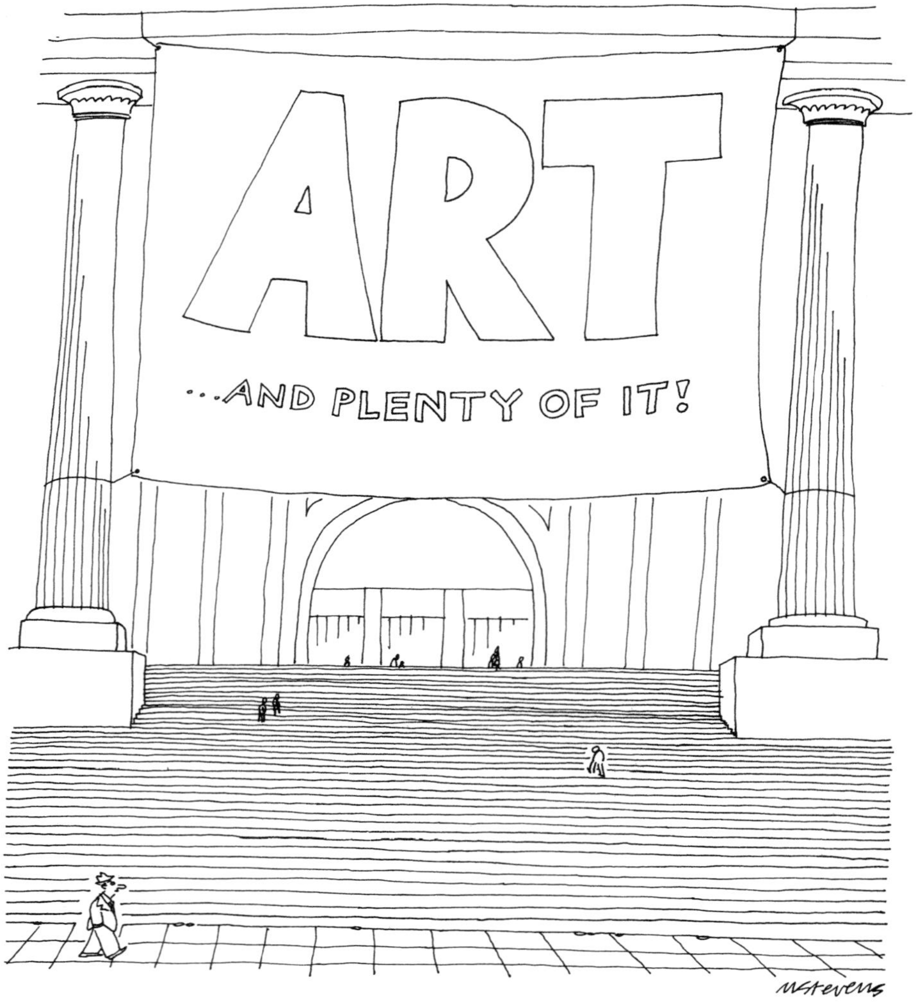
ART
...AND PLENTY OF IT!

"I'll be all right in a minute. I'm afraid I accelerated on the way down."

Richter

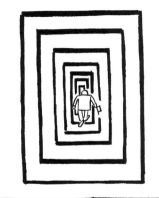

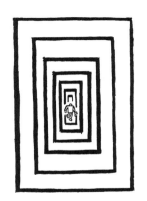

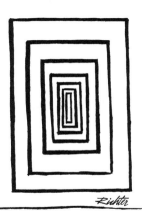

"I would like a tube of lemon yellow, cadmium red, cobalt blue, ivory, black, and zinc white, a sixteen-by-twenty canvas, a couple of brushes, and that book 'Painting in Oils.'"

"Get that de Kooning sneer off your face. This is Turner!"

"Pretty bad, isn't it?"

"I don't know anything about art, but this is a damned good Martini."

"*Don't click me. I'm just here to buy cards.*"

"I was grinding out barnyards and farmhouses and cows in the meadow, and then, suddenly, I figured to hell with it."

"Grandma Moses doesn't get into a funk. Grandma Moses doesn't have to wait for the creative yeast. Grandma Moses isn't hamstrung by the tensions of her time. Grandma Moses knocks them out one after another. Grandma Moses…"

"*Maybe someday we could set aside a cave just for art.*"

"I know the type. All you'd ever get out of him would be 'We can't afford it'!"

"'To Mario—Good food, good fun. Thanks. Leonardo da Vinci.'"

"*I hear you've been doing exciting things with eggs and dye.*"

"Why can't someone design a museum that doesn't have to be explained?"

"'Plastic Study of Vertical Planes.' Who does he think he's kidding?"

"Has it said anything to you yet?"

INDEX OF ARTISTS

Wait!

The laughs don't stop there!

Check out these other hilarious collections from

Bloomberg
PRESS

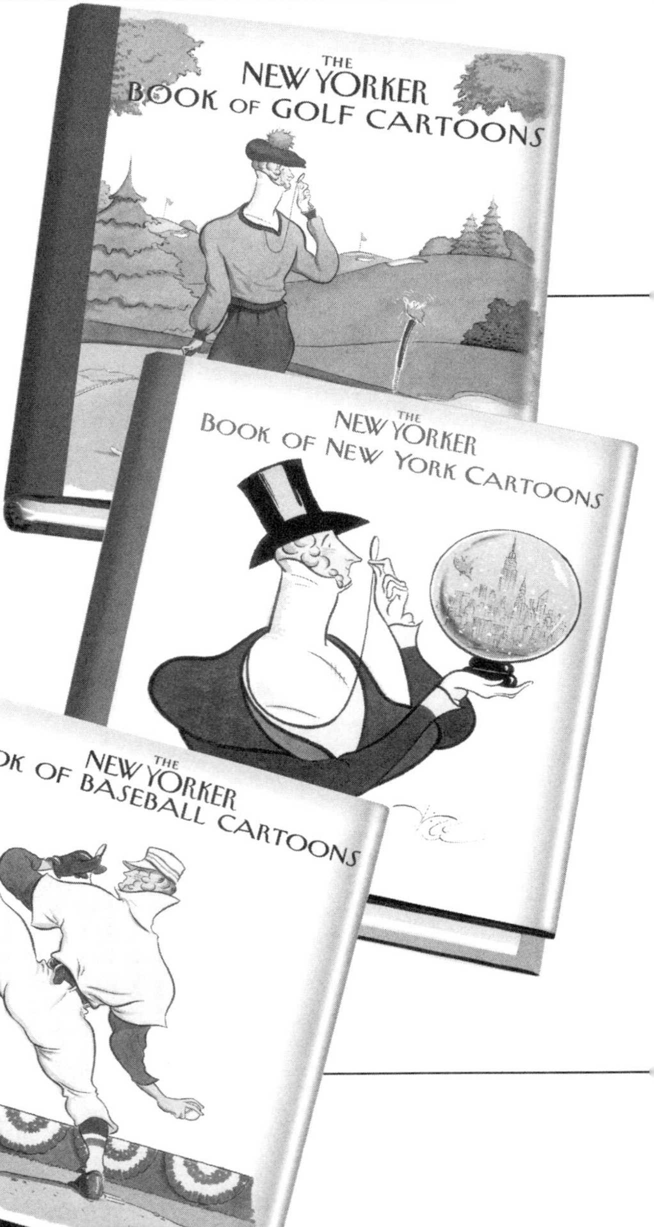

THE NEW YORKER BOOK OF GOLF CARTOONS
THE NEW YORKER BOOK OF NEW YORK CARTOONS

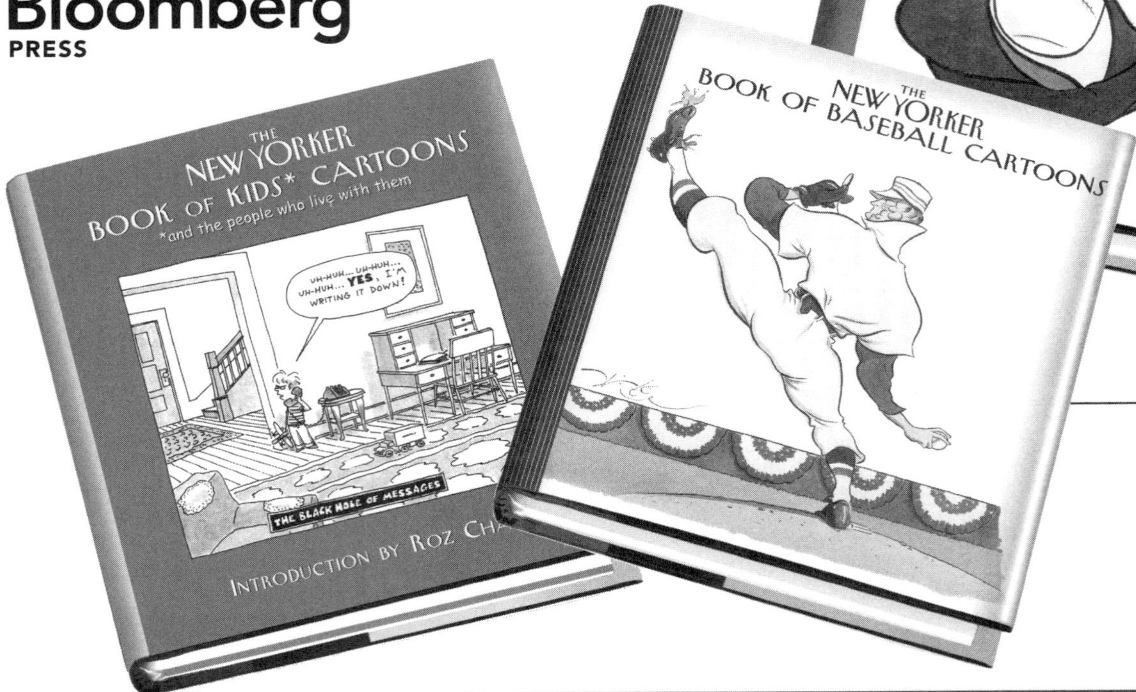

THE NEW YORKER BOOK OF KIDS* CARTOONS
*and the people who live with them
UH-HUH... UH-HUH... UH-HUH... YES, I'M WRITING IT DOWN!
THE BLACK HOLE OF MESSAGES
INTRODUCTION BY ROZ CH
THE NEW YORKER BOOK OF BASEBALL CARTOONS

Available where books are sold or at www.bloomberg.com/books.

FEELING ARTISTIC?

BUILD YOUR OWN ART GALLERY WITH CARTOON AND COVER ART FROM THE NEW YORKER.

Find your favorite *New Yorker* cartoon or cover, on anything from business to pleasure, by browsing our extensive online archive at **www.cartoonbank.com**.

Mario Micossi March 6, 1965 ALL COVERS ARE FULL COLOR

"Artsy. But not fartsy."

Jack Ziegler January 17, 1994

NEW YORKER COVER PRINTS

Every cover in our Vintage Collection, 1925 to 1992, represents an exquisite moment in time. From simple and sublime, to bold and playful, each one is a little masterpiece. Over 3,000 to choose from. Find your favorite artist, subject, or select a *New Yorker* cover with a special date. Available framed and unframed, large and magazine sized.

NEW YORKER CARTOON PRINTS

Virtually every cartoon ever published in *The New Yorker* is available as a framed or matted print. Hang them up in your home or office. A great way to make a statement . . . or just to make someone laugh.

ALSO AVAILABLE: BOOKS, SHIRTS, GIFTS AND MORE!

CARTOONBANK.COM
A New Yorker Magazine Company

VISIT WWW.CARTOONBANK.COM OR CALL 1-800-897-TOON